THE CIVIL WAR

EARLY BATTLES OF THE CIVIL WAR

by Kelsey Jopp

FOCUS
READERS®

VOYAGER

www.focusreaders.com

Focus Readers is distributed by North Star Editions:
sales@northstareditions.com | 888-417-0195

Produced for Focus Readers by Red Line Editorial.

Content Consultant: Dr. Gideon Mailer, Associate Professor of History, University of Minnesota Duluth

Photographs ©: E. & H.T. Anthony/Brady's National Photographic Portrait Galleries/Library of Congress, cover, 1; George N. Barnard/Civil War Photographs, 1861–1865/Library of Congress, 4–5; Red Line Editorial, 6, 30, 36; Everett Historical/Shutterstock Images, 8–9, 25, 33, 34–35, 41, 42–43, 44; Library of Congress, 11, 14–15; Barnard & Gibson/Library of Congress, 13; Union View Co./The Robin G. Stanford Collection/Library of Congress, 16; James F. Gibson/Civil War Photographs, 1861–1865/Library of Congress, 19, 26–27; George Armistead/AP Images, 20–21; Civil War Photographs, 1861–1865/Library of Congress, 22; Mathew B. Brady/AP Images, 29; Alexander Gardner/Library of Congress, 38

Library of Congress Cataloging-in-Publication Data
Names: Jopp, Kelsey, 1993- author.
Title: Early battles of the Civil War / by Kelsey Jopp.
Description: Lake Elmo, MN : Focus Readers, 2020. | Series: The Civil War |
   Includes bibliographical references and index. | Audience: Grades 7-9
Identifiers: LCCN 2019036406 (print) | LCCN 2019036407 (ebook) | ISBN
   9781644930793 (hardcover) | ISBN 9781644931585 (paperback) | ISBN
   9781644933169 (pdf) | ISBN 9781644932377 (ebook)
Subjects: LCSH: United States--History--Civil War,
   1861-1865--Campaigns--Juvenile literature.
Classification: LCC E470 .J77 2020 (print) | LCC E470 (ebook) | DDC
   973.7/3--dc23
LC record available at https://lccn.loc.gov/2019036406
LC ebook record available at https://lccn.loc.gov/2019036407

Printed in the United States of America
Mankato, MN
012020

ABOUT THE AUTHOR

Kelsey Jopp is an editor, writer, and lifelong learner. She lives in Saint Paul, Minnesota, where she enjoys practicing yoga and playing endless fetch with her sheltie, Teddy.

TABLE OF CONTENTS

CHAPTER 1

SHOTS FIRED

On April 11, 1861, a small boat began crossing the harbor near Charleston, South Carolina. It carried messengers from the Confederate States of America. At the time, seven states belonged to the Confederacy. These states had **seceded** from the United States after Abraham Lincoln's election in 1860. After leaving the Union, the states requested control of any US military property on their land. However, President Lincoln refused.

Fort Sumter (in the distance) was a US fort in the state of South Carolina.

A growing divide over slavery had led up to this conflict. Slavery spread to America in the 1600s. By the early 1800s, most Northern states prohibited it. Some opponents of slavery were abolitionists. They believed slavery was wrong. But many people were against slavery for

OPPOSING SIDES (JUNE 1861)

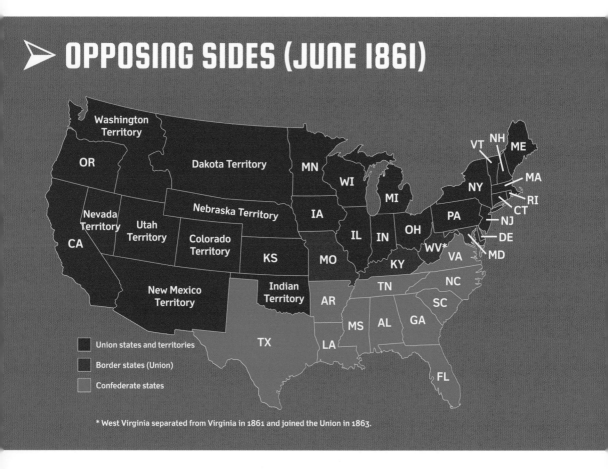

* West Virginia separated from Virginia in 1861 and joined the Union in 1863.

economic reasons. They thought it gave Southern farms an unfair advantage.

Lincoln was against the expansion of slavery, but he wasn't an abolitionist. He feared the divide over the issue would break up the nation. When the proslavery states seceded, the threat of war became all the more real.

Now, the boat was carrying Confederate messengers to Fort Sumter. This fort stood in the harbor outside Charleston. When the messengers reached the fort, they told the federal troops to leave. But the fort's commander wouldn't give in.

On April 12, the messengers returned with a warning. If the federal troops did not leave in the next hour, the Confederates would open fire. When the commander refused, the Confederates attacked. On April 14, the federal soldiers finally surrendered. The Civil War had begun.

CHAPTER 2

THE BATTLE OF BULL RUN

After the Battle of Fort Sumter, many people in the Union demanded action. They wanted to make a move against the Confederacy. Lincoln even called for 75,000 recruits to serve in the Union army. However, the leader of the army advised Lincoln to wait. He feared the volunteer troops were not ready for battle.

That summer, the political pressure on Lincoln continued to grow. Soon, he had little choice.

Union cavalrymen ride near Bull Run, a creek in Virginia.

In July, he ordered Union forces to attack the Confederate army in Virginia. The attack would open a path to Richmond. This city served as the Confederate capital. Union forces planned to take the city and end the war quickly.

On July 16, 1861, Union general Irvin McDowell followed Lincoln's orders. His 35,000 soldiers left the Union capital of Washington, DC. They marched toward Bull Run, a small creek in northern Virginia. Stationed behind the creek were 20,000 Confederate soldiers led by General P. G. T. Beauregard.

Beauregard's men prepared to attack McDowell's left **flank**. This attack would move the Confederates toward Centreville, Virginia. There, they would cut off the Union forces from Washington, DC. Beauregard called for backup to help pull off this **maneuver**.

⬆ Irvin McDowell (fifth from right) stands with his commanding officers.

Meanwhile, McDowell was unaware of Beauregard's plan. So, he also planned to attack on the left. If both armies attacked the other's left, they would simply circle each other. Neither attack would succeed.

On July 21, the generals put their plans into action. McDowell moved first, giving the Union a lead. At 5:30 a.m., the Union fired the first shot. Within a few hours, the battle was well underway.

When Beauregard heard the sounds of battle, he changed course. Instead of attacking McDowell's left, he focused on defense.

The Union forces pushed the Confederates back for two hours. But the battle turned when the Confederate backup came. General Thomas J. Jackson formed a defensive line against the Union. Though he took a shot through the hand, he didn't back down. Another general noted that Jackson stood like a stone wall. After that, he became known as "Stonewall" Jackson.

As more backup arrived, the Confederates launched a counterattack. The soldiers roared as they attacked, introducing the famous Rebel Yell. After much back and forth, the Confederates finally broke through the Union's right flank. At the peak of the battle, Colonel J. E. B. Stuart arrived. His men charged the Union troops and

The Battle of Bull Run took place in a field near this house.

forced them to retreat. By July 22, the defeated Union forces had returned to Washington, DC.

The Union suffered nearly 3,000 **casualties** in the Battle of Bull Run. On the Confederate side, approximately 1,900 soldiers were dead or wounded. In just one day, the Union's hope for a quick war had ended. And the Confederates were all the more expectant of victory.

CHAPTER 3

ON LAND AND SEA

After the Battle of Bull Run, the Confederates won battles at Wilson's Creek in Missouri and Ball's Bluff in Virginia. As the Confederacy's strength became evident, the Union worked to improve its army. Lincoln replaced McDowell with General George McClellan, who quickly began training his troops.

In early 1862, the Union army won two key battles in the West. Both occurred in Tennessee.

A newspaper illustration shows Union troops retreating during the Battle of Ball's Bluff.

▲ The Confederates used ships known as blockade runners to sneak past Union forces and into Southern harbors.

These victories put the Union in control of two important rivers. Controlling these rivers was part of the Union's plan to surround and trap the Confederacy. The Confederates would run out of supplies if they did not have access to waterways.

The previous year, the Union navy had formed a **blockade** around Southern ports. More than 500 Union ships stopped supplies from reaching these harbors. With no way to send goods or supplies, Southern trade suffered.

Battles along this coast marked a major change in naval warfare. Prior to the Civil War, the United

States had used wooden ships. Explosives could easily damage or sink them. So, people began covering ships with iron. The Union navy built its first ironclad for the war in 1861. It was named the USS *Monitor.*

The Confederacy had to build its own navy. When Virginia seceded in 1861, it acquired the USS *Merrimack.* This wooden ship had belonged to the US Navy. But when Virginia seceded, the navy burned and sank the ship. The Union didn't want the Confederacy to use it. Nevertheless, the Confederates saved the ship and covered it in iron. They renamed it the CSS *Virginia.*

THINK ABOUT IT ◄

Both armies tried to cut off the other's supplies. How would doing this help them win the war?

On March 8, 1862, the CSS *Virginia* attacked a Union **fleet** at Hampton Roads. This harbor is just off the coast of Virginia. During the battle, the Confederates destroyed two Union ships. That evening, however, the USS *Monitor* arrived. The next morning, the *Virginia* continued its attack. Crowds of supporters for both sides watched from the shore. The *Monitor* soon entered the conflict, and the two ships exchanged fire.

The crews of both ships were inexperienced. As a result, they struggled to do serious damage. Eventually, the *Virginia* hit the *Monitor*'s pilothouse. This room was where the commander steered the ship. When it was hit, iron splinters flew into the commander's eyes. The injury should have given the Confederates an advantage. However, the *Virginia* was low on ammunition. Its commander decided to sail away.

After the Battle of Hampton Roads, the USS *Monitor* had just a few small dents.

Both sides claimed victory at the Battle of Hampton Roads. The Union believed the *Monitor* had won since the *Virginia* had retreated. The Confederates, on the other hand, were pleased with the *Virginia*'s performance. They had hopes of breaking the Union's blockade. Although the battle was a draw, it went down in history. As the first battle between ironclad ships, it paved the way for further naval progress.

CHAPTER 4

THE BATTLE OF SHILOH

In February 1862, after capturing Fort Donelson in Tennessee, Union troops moved south. Eventually, they hoped to enter Mississippi. That way, they could take full control of the Mississippi River. In April, the troops camped near Shiloh Church in Pittsburg Landing, Tennessee. Their commander, General Ulysses S. Grant, was waiting for backup. Then they would advance on Confederate general Albert Sidney Johnston.

Drummer boys gather near a tent at a Union army camp in early 1862.

Like many Confederate generals, Albert Sidney Johnston had previously served in the US Army.

However, Johnston was aware of Grant's location and plan. He decided to attack before Grant's backup could arrive. Because the Union was planning an **offensive**, Johnston knew that Grant would not be expecting an attack.

But Johnston's troops weren't prepared either. His 45,000 men were camped at Corinth, Mississippi. Johnston's order to attack Grant had to be acted on quickly. Most of his troops began marching while the order was still being written.

However, one general wouldn't march without a written order. He refused to move his 10,000 men. The other 35,000 soldiers struggled to march around them. By the time the full army could move, it had lost precious time.

The march didn't improve from there. A rainstorm caused the already muddy roads to flood. During the night, entire **regiments** got lost. By morning, the regiments were a tangled mess.

Despite this chaos, the Union army remained unaware of Johnston's plan. Union troops in the front were the first to see the Confederate soldiers. They quickly spread word of an attack.

THINK ABOUT IT ◁

Do you think speed or strategy is more important to winning battles? Why?

But others weren't convinced. One Union general threatened to arrest the men for spreading false news. On April 5, a Union commander sent out a search. He found Confederate soldiers the next morning. Once they had been seen, the soldiers opened fire. The Battle of Shiloh had begun.

On the morning of April 6, the Confederates pushed back the Union's left and right flanks. In the afternoon, the battle centered on the Hornet's Nest. This was an area of road under Union control. The Confederates put all their energy toward it. Johnston received a fatal wound in the process. By the end of the day, the Confederates won the Hornet's Nest. But their commander had died, and the troops were tired.

Union backup arrived on the morning of April 7. The reorganized troops began driving the Confederates back. The Union recaptured

⚐ During the Battle of Shiloh, each side suffered more than 10,000 casualties.

the Hornet's Nest by late morning. And in late afternoon, the Confederates retreated.

The Battle of Shiloh was the bloodiest battle in American history up to that point. The Union won, but not without problems. During the battle, 10,000 of Grant's men had run away. Another division didn't even fight the first day. The South was even more discouraged. It had lost Johnston, one of its strongest commanders. It had also failed to stop the Union from entering Mississippi.

CHAPTER 5

BATTLES FOR RICHMOND

In the spring of 1862, Union armies advanced on several fronts. The largest of these armies belonged to McClellan. He began his Peninsula Campaign in March. McClellan hoped to capture Richmond. Like the ports and the Mississippi River, this city was key to Union strategy. Without access to waterways, the Confederacy would run out of supplies. And without its capital city, it would have no center of operation.

George McClellan's forces in Virginia included artillery pulled by horses.

To get to Richmond, McClellan would pass through the Virginia Peninsula. The peninsula sat between the York and James Rivers. Taking this route would allow the Union navy to move and defend McClellan's troops.

As McClellan moved his large army, the Confederates launched their own campaign. Stonewall Jackson led his troops into the Shenandoah Valley. This valley stretched from Harpers Ferry to Roanoke, Virginia. Between February and June, Jackson's men fought six battles there. Union forces that could have helped McClellan were busy fighting Jackson.

Eventually, the last of McClellan's men entered the Virginia Peninsula. But once there, the troops faced delays. McClellan received false information about the Confederate army. He thought General Joseph E. Johnston had more forces than he did.

▲ The Battle of Seven Pines was also called the Battle of Fair Oaks.

As a result, McClellan moved cautiously. He even pulled back several times.

The Battle of Seven Pines created another delay. This battle began on May 31. It took place only 6 miles (9.7 km) from Richmond. Johnston's men tried to drive McClellan back from the city. The Union troops managed to hold their ground. But the battle negatively affected McClellan's campaign.

During the battle, General Johnston was badly wounded. Robert E. Lee took his place. Lee was aggressive. When McClellan reached Richmond three weeks later, Lee did not hold back. He called for help from Jackson's army, which had finished its campaign in the Shenandoah Valley. Together, the two generals attacked McClellan. They pushed him away from Richmond in a series of several

➤ SEVEN DAYS' BATTLES

June 25
Battle of
Oak Grove

June 26
Battle of
Beaver
Dam Creek

June 27
Battles of
Gaines's Mill
and Garnett's
Farm

June 28
Battle of
Golding's Farm

June 29
Battle of
Savage's Station

June 30
Battles of Glendale
and White Oak
Swamp

July 1
Battle of
Malvern Hill

battles. This stretch of fighting became known as the Seven Days' Battles. Soon after, McClellan retreated toward Washington, DC. The Peninsula Campaign was over.

The battles around Richmond changed the course of the war. One major impact was the Confederates' decision to replace Johnston with Lee. Without Lee, the Confederates could have lost their capital city. Lee went on to win several other battles in the East. His success boosted Southern **morale**.

For the Union, the losses at Richmond were devastating. As the Confederate capital, Richmond was essential to winning the war. If Richmond fell, the Confederacy could fall. But the campaign had failed. And all the fighting had hardened both armies. Neither side planned to give in any time soon.

ROBERT E. LEE

Robert E. Lee was born on January 19, 1807. He grew up in Virginia. His family was highly respected there. His father had been a hero in the American Revolutionary War (1775–1783). Lee followed in his footsteps, serving in the army for many years. In 1859, Lincoln called on him to stop a raid at Harpers Ferry, Virginia. Lee succeeded.

Two years later, Lincoln asked Lee to command the Union forces. Lee declined the offer when Virginia left the Union. Out of loyalty to his state, Lee fought for the Confederacy instead.

Lee was a strong and daring general. But when it came to slavery, he had concerning views. On the one hand, Lee believed slavery was wrong. In a letter to his wife, he called slavery "an evil in any country."[1] But he also said it was "a greater evil to the white man than to the black race."[2] Like many others, Lee seemed to care more about white

 Even after the Civil War ended, Robert E. Lee opposed giving formerly enslaved people the right to vote.

people's success than black people's freedom. He even wrote that slavery was "necessary for [black people's] instruction."[3]

Today, Lee is remembered for his military skill. Many historians consider him the greatest general of the Confederate army. However, they also recognize his racist views.

1. Elizabeth Brown Pryor. *Reading the Man: A Portrait of Robert E. Lee Through His Private Letters*. New York: Viking, 2007. 144–145.
2. Pryor. *Reading the Man*. 145.
3. Pryor. *Reading the Man*. 144.

CHAPTER 6

THE MARYLAND CAMPAIGN

In the summer of 1862, Lincoln began drafting the Emancipation Proclamation. If this order was successful, it would free enslaved people in Confederate states. But Lincoln wasn't ready to release it. He wanted to wait for the Union to win a battle. Then the order would be easier to enforce.

Confederate leaders also wanted a strategic victory. In early September, Lee sent Jackson with half his army to capture Harpers Ferry, Virginia.

President Abraham Lincoln (left) and General McClellan meet on a battlefield.

This would open a route to bring supplies to Lee's men. Afterward, Jackson and Lee planned to reunite and invade the North. Lee's target was the border state of Maryland. Border states were loyal to the Union but allowed slavery. By invading

➤ THE MARYLAND CAMPAIGN

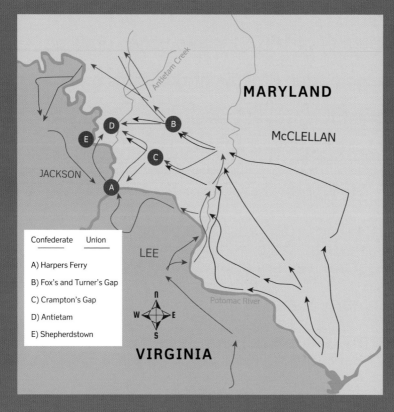

MARYLAND

McCLELLAN

Antietam Creek

JACKSON

LEE

Potomac River

VIRGINIA

Confederate   Union

A) Harpers Ferry
B) Fox's and Turner's Gap
C) Crampton's Gap
D) Antietam
E) Shepherdstown

Maryland, Lee hoped the state would join the Confederacy.

Lee's plan to invade Maryland was titled Special Orders No. 191. He gave copies of the order to various generals. At the time, McClellan knew Lee was planning an invasion. But he didn't know the details. To be safe, he had his troops spread out. McClellan's men moved northwest as they pushed the Confederates back.

One day, a Union soldier found a lost copy of Lee's order. It was lying in a meadow, wrapped around cigars. The lost order gave McClellan the details he needed. With Jackson at Harpers Ferry, Lee's army was divided. McClellan took the opportunity to attack.

On September 17, Union troops slowly made their way through a cornfield near Antietam Creek. Tall cornstalks hid the Union soldiers.

This sunken road became known as Bloody Lane because so many people died there.

Less than 600 feet (180 m) away, Confederate soldiers waited. They lay on their stomachs, guns ready. As the Union soldiers emerged from the corn, the battle began.

Next, the Union forces headed for a sunken road. However, more than 2,000 Confederate soldiers were hiding in the road. As the Union flank appeared, the Confederates fired. They took out nearly every soldier in the front line. But the remaining Union soldiers surrounded the road.

Before long, most of the Confederates inside were dead or wounded.

The final stage of fighting took place at Antietam Creek. Beside the creek was a steep bluff where Confederates hid. To reach them, the Union troops had to cross a stone bridge. Facing heavy gunfire, they took three hours to cross. By the time they climbed the bluffs, Lee had called for backup. The reinforced Confederates pushed back the Union troops.

After 12 hours of fighting, the armies suffered approximately 23,000 casualties. Neither army had gained much ground. The next day, Lee pulled his army and retreated south. Lincoln ordered McClellan to pursue Lee, but the general refused. Later, McClellan would face criticism for this decision. Even so, the Union considered Lee's retreat a success.

GEORGE McCLELLAN

George McClellan was born on December 3, 1826, in Philadelphia, Pennsylvania. He began his military training when he was only 16 years old. Four years later, he graduated second in his class.

McClellan's military duties grew with the start of the Civil War. After the Union defeat at Bull Run, he became commander of the Army of the Potomac. Although he was popular with his troops, McClellan faced criticism for his command style. Lincoln believed McClellan was too cautious.

McClellan's greatest errors came at the Battle of Antietam. After finding Lee's lost order, McClellan was confident. He wrote to Lincoln: "I think Lee has made a gross mistake, and he will be severely punished for it."[1]

McClellan formed a strong bond with his men, earning the nickname "Little Mac."

McClellan planned to act quickly. "I have the whole rebel force in front of me," he wrote. "No time shall be lost."[2] However, he thought the Confederate army was larger than it was. Though he spoke confidently, he acted cautiously. He gained hardly any ground in the battle. And at the end, he let Lee retreat. Today, McClellan is largely remembered for his mistakes.

1. George Brinton McClellan. *The Civil War Papers of George B. McClellan: Selected Correspondence, 1860–1865*. Edited by Stephen W. Sears. New York: Ticknor and Fields, 1989. 453.
2. McClellan. *Civil War Papers*. 453.

CHAPTER 7

THE WAR CONTINUES

E ven though neither side gained much ground at the Battle of Antietam, it was a strategic victory for the Union. The Union army had stopped Lee from entering Maryland. The battle also gave the Union a boost in morale. With that in mind, Lincoln believed the time was right to issue the Emancipation Proclamation. This order declared that all enslaved people in Confederate states would be free as of January 1, 1863.

Lincoln's Emancipation Proclamation did not apply to areas under Union control.

▲ Black soldiers fire their rifles during fighting at Dutch Gap Canal in 1864.

The Emancipation Proclamation shifted the focus of the war. Previously, Lincoln's main goal had been to keep the Union together. But with the proclamation, ending slavery became another important war aim.

The Union army also began recruiting black soldiers. At the start of the war, black people were not allowed to serve in the US military. Lincoln thought border states might secede if he lifted this ban. But as the war progressed, the number of white volunteers fell. The proclamation allowed black soldiers to enlist. By the end of the war, nearly 200,000 black men fought for the Union.

The war took many turns over the next three years. However, the early battles of the war left a mark. They gave rise to leaders such as Lee and Grant. These battles also ended hopes of a quick, easy war. The conflicts at Shiloh and Antietam were some of the war's bloodiest. Their casualties shocked the nation. It became clear that victory, and even failure, would come at great cost.

THINK ABOUT IT ◁

When the war began, Lincoln had no plans to end slavery. Later, he issued the Emancipation Proclamation. Do you think it's okay for leaders to change their minds? Why or why not?

FOCUS ON
EARLY BATTLES OF THE CIVIL WAR

Write your answers on a separate piece of paper.

1. Write a paragraph that describes the main ideas of Chapter 5.

2. Do you think the Union or the Confederacy had more success in the early battles of the Civil War? Why?

3. Which conflict ended McClellan's Peninsula Campaign?

    A. the Battle of Shiloh
    B. the Battle of Seven Pines
    C. the Seven Days' Battles

4. At Antietam Creek, why did the Confederate troops hide out on the bluff?

    A. so they could easily escape the battle
    B. so they could attack the Union from above
    C. so they could have access to drinking water

Answer key on page 48.

GLOSSARY

blockade
When an area is closed off so nothing can go in or out.

casualties
People who are killed, wounded, or missing in battle.

economic
Relating to the distribution of goods, services, and money.

flank
The right or left side of a military line.

fleet
A group of warships under one command.

maneuver
A series of actions a military takes against enemy forces.

morale
The mood of a group of people, especially people in a difficult situation.

offensive
An attack made by a military to gain territory or take control of a target.

regiments
Military units that are made up of large groups of soldiers.

seceded
Formally withdrew from a political group or nation.

TO LEARN MORE

BOOKS

Grayson, Robert. *The U.S. Civil War: Why They Fought*. North Mankato, MN: Capstone, 2016.

Kenney, Karen Latchana. *Abraham Lincoln's Presidency*. Minneapolis: Lerner Publications, 2017.

Otfinoski, Steven. *The Split History of the Battle of Fort Sumter*. North Mankato, MN: Capstone, 2018.

NOTE TO EDUCATORS

Visit **www.focusreaders.com** to find lesson plans, activities, links, and other resources related to this title.

INDEX

Answer Key: 1. Answers will vary; **2.** Answers will vary; **3.** C; **4.** B